Contents

33

Scripture-Based Ideas for REACHING OUT TO OTHERS

Pat King

ONE LIGUORI DRIVE
LIGUORI, MO 63057-9999
(314) 464-2500

ISBN 0-89243-451-1
Library of Congress Catalog Card Number: 92-82794

Printed in United States of America

Cover design by Chris Sharp

Introduction

There are eight people sitting in your living room. Let's say there are nine different categories in which they can use their time and talents to reach out to others. That makes seventy-two different helping approaches. But wait, each of those approaches will be influenced by the personality of the helper. So that's eight times seventy-two or five hundred seventy-six different ways those eight people can reach out to others. Each of their levels of compassion is different as well: eight times five hundred seventy-six....

You can see that writing a study on reaching out to others has its challenges. I can't tell you how to help others; only you can decide that. God has formed you individually with your own gifts and circumstances. But I can share some Scripture with you, tell you what Jesus said and did, and give you some ideas. I can also help you guard against doing so much that your energy gets eaten up.

As you work through *Scripture-Based Ideas for Reaching Out to Others,* your responses, ideas, and choices will be unique. After all, God's plan for you is unlike any other. May this study enable you to reach out to others in ways that are uniquely yours.

One word of...well...I'll call it warning. The first lesson is different from the rest: it's longer and more complicated.

Stick with it; it challenges you to discover more about yourself. In that way, it lays the foundation for the rest of the study.

Plan to work on the study weekly. Every Thursday evening, Monday morning, or Sunday afternoon, allow half an hour—or more—to do one lesson. Then pray about that lesson during the week. Have fun with it. Let it speak to you, expand you, comfort you, for your sake and the sake of everyone in your life.

What to Expect

Each lesson begins with a Scripture quote and "Beginning Prayer" that reflect the theme for that particular lesson. Don't rush through this section. As you begin each lesson, ask the Holy Spirit to help you.

"The Lesson" follows the Scripture citation and prayer. This section offers comments, stories, and insights that center on the theme and offer a deeper appreciation for that specific method of reaching out to others.

The section titled "Personal Application" offers you the opportunity to creatively reflect on the theme in ways that apply to your daily life: in your home, your community, and the world.

"Wrap Up" consists of six specific suggestions for the week ahead:

Continue during the week: It's important to share something from each lesson with someone else. Ideally, the person you share with does the study with you.

Gift Assessment Chart: At the end of each lesson, take a minute to fill in the chart beginning on page 124. When you're finished with all the lessons, your notes on the chart will give you a clear picture of yourself and your specific gifts for reaching out to others.

Especially for you: Every week do something for yourself. Because reaching out to others takes a lot of energy, make caring for you one of your priorities.

Just for fun: This is for those who may forget to have a little fun.

Journal: You'll need a special notebook for this. All your journal writing is private. Punctuation, grammar, and spelling do not matter. Write as much or as little as you want. Getting your thoughts down is what's important. Many people find that keeping a journal helps them discover a great deal about themselves and their relationships. You will be given a starter-thought for direction and inspiration.

Memorize: It's important to have the Scriptures in our memory banks. Put the weekly verses on note cards and tape them on the bathroom mirror. You'll learn them easily and bless the rest of the household by giving them a new Scripture to look at each week as they brush their teeth.

Each lesson ends with "Closing Prayer," acknowledging the most important part of reaching out to others: that what we need most is the grace of God.

Lesson One
The Way You Are Made

I praise you, so wonderfully you made me;
wonderful are your works!
Psalm 139:14

Beginning Prayer

Dear God, the world, it seems, cries out in distress. How can I, so limited in so many ways, reach out to those in need? Please show me, through the Holy Spirit and the pages of this study, what your special role is for me.

Glory to the Father, and to the Son, and to the Holy Spirit; as it was in the beginning, is now, and will be for ever. Amen.

The Lesson:
Reaching Out to Others
for the Right Reasons

"There's a woman in desperate need of help." Father outlined the situation. "She has two children, her husband has just died, and her money is scarce."

"What can we do?" came the collective question from the twelve couples who made up our parish's young-marrieds group.

"Her house: it really needs work. Gutters, downspouts—and something needs to be done about the kitchen."

Some of the men went to the woman's home to have a look. Indeed, the gutters needed work and the kitchen was old. "Actually," said one of the men, "things aren't as bad as they are at my house." Father pointed out that fixing up the house was our Christian duty. The gutters and downspouts were replaced. Next came the kitchen. My husband, Bill, who hadn't worked on the gutters, started feeling pressured by the rest of the group to do his share of the work. Father had located a new sink and cabinets and insisted, again, that our responsibility was to widows and orphans; not helping the widow would be going against God's will.

That summer Bill and I were expecting our eighth child, we had just moved to a larger house, and there was much to be done to get settled. I remember that Saturday morning when Bill sat at the kitchen table and said, "I really don't want to go work on that kitchen, but I don't know what to do. I need to stay here and work on our own home, but Dick, with more family responsibilities than I have, is helping. So is Bob, whose own house is unfinished. How can I let them down?"

I wanted Bill at home, too, but Father's admonitions resounded in the back of our minds. If Bill didn't go, would we be selfishly letting down the widow—and God?

Reluctantly, Bill left. When he returned late that night, I knew something was wrong. "It was a big mistake to go. The widow wanted us to move the sink and window that they just put in last week. That meant we had to undo everything that was already done. She isn't happy with anything." Bill paused. "My place was here. I was wrong to go and help out on something I knew all along wasn't for me."

That was many years ago, but the experience provides a window into the purpose of this chapter. As you read and study this book on reaching out to help others, it's vital to remember that your decisions have to be based on your own values rather than the commands of someone else. Failing to consider your own beliefs, gifts, and situations when deciding to help others is to take a shortcut. And ultimately, shortcuts lessen your achievement and leave you feeling unfulfilled.

Bill and I both knew that working on the widow's home was not for us at that time. But we weren't guided by our own values. Rather, we listened to the voice of authority and the pressure of others—who, by the way, also became disillusioned.

We wanted to please God, a worthy goal. But we took a shortcut. We tried to reach a goal by pleasing Father and friends. Too often, Christians set out with noble aims but use a shortcut to get there.

The Temptation to Take a Shortcut

The purpose of this entire endeavor is to help you decide what you want to aim for in reaching out to others and then help you find the most fulfilling way to go about it. We begin with Scripture.

Read Genesis 2:15-17. What is the one rule that God makes clear to Adam?

___

Then Eve comes on the scene, and Adam tells her what God has said.

Read Genesis 3:1-5. Listen to the shortcut Eve is offered. What is the offer?

___

Read Genesis 3:6-7. What do you think was Eve's big mistake?

____

____

Eating the fruit? Yes. But more than that; Eve's mistake was listening to and believing the wrong voice. How do you think Adam and Eve felt after taking this shortcut?

____

____

In the New Testament, Jesus tells a story that may be even more familiar to today's families than to the people who first heard it.

Read Luke 15:11-18. What was the son's aim when he left home with his inheritance? Reflect on your own aims (or those of your children or friends) when you headed—at last—away from the confines of home.

____

____

What shortcuts did the son take to realize his goal?

____

____

How, do you think, did the son feel about the outcome of his shortcut?

____

____

Following is one of the most infamous shortcuts in history.

Read Matthew 27:19-26, Mark 15:15, and Luke 23:20-25.

What is Pilate convinced of? ____________________

What does he do anyway? ____________________

Why? ____________________

How, do you think, did Pilate feel afterward?

____

Scripture tells us that shortly after Jesus' crucifixion, Pilate was called to Rome. He spent the entire voyage calling for basins of water so he could continually wash his hands.

Scripture records the all-time great shortcut offer.

Read Matthew 4:8-11. Satan transported Jesus to a place where he could see all the nations of the world and their glory: Jerusalem, the United States, Russia, Europe, the Third World countries, all of China, every nation that existed or would ever exist. It was all Satan's territory. Ever since the great Eden episode, Satan had been the prince of this world, and in this account he makes the most incredible offer. What does he offer Jesus?

____

____

With all the nations in full view, Satan proceeded with his offer to Jesus: "All these I shall give to you, if you will prostrate yourself and worship me." Satan craves worship, but it was a daring proposition to put to the Son of God.

Jesus understood. If he worshiped Satan, he would not have to go the way of the cross: suffering, rejection, and death. He had the opportunity to take the easy way out, to compromise, to take a shortcut.

Jesus was tempted. Noted author and theologian Dietrich Bonhoeffer describes the offer as immeasurably bright, beautiful, and alluring. How did Jesus respond to this temptation to take a shortcut?

____

____

____

How, do you think, did Jesus feel deep within himself after he refused Satan's offer?

____

____

____

Why Is the Shortcut Attractive?

If the long way around is the best choice, why does the shortcut seem so attractive? To understand, let's take a much-simplified look at our basic makeup. According to Richard Gula in his book *To Walk Together Again: The Sacrament of Reconciliation* (Paulist Press, 1984), "Every human personality is composed of the id and the ego. The id is the unconscious reservoir of instinctual drives dominated by the pleasure principle. This is the area of our lives that is beneath the surface. It directs us, even though we can't consciously deal with all it contains. The ego is our conscious structure. It mediates the forces of the id with the demands of society and the reality of the physical world," Gala explains.

For example, I may have an unconscious desire to hide whenever a certain neighbor approaches the front door. This could be because the approaching person reminds me of a long-buried time of pain. However, my ego steps in and answers the door because that's the socially acceptable thing to do. (If the id is feeling a great deal of pain, the ego may not be able to override it. But in normal situations, the ego will answer the door.)

This is one of the many ways we are fearfully and wonderfully made (Psalm 139). Since the human personality cannot begin to understand and sort out all of life's situations and traumas, it buries them below the conscious. This keeps the conscious free to deal with the demands of living and to make the necessary choices: *Yes, I feel uncomfortable when this neighbor comes to the door because I know he's angry over something. But I will answer the door and get it over with and choose, with the grace of God, to love him by being nice to him.*

This is a normal and good way for the human personality to make choices. However, problems arise when our choices are made by the superego rather than the ego. The ego of someone else is superimposed on our own ego to regulate our conduct by using guilt. Rather than listening to our own wisdom, we hear the voices of parents, teachers, civil authorities, the boss, the priest, the grade-school nuns, and so forth. Gula says that the "...voice of the superego tells us we are good when we do what we are told and that we are bad [and thus feel guilty] when we do not do what the authority tells us."

The voice of the superego usually says "you should" or "you have to." When Bill and I struggled with how to help the widow, we listened to the voice of our superego. The priest said we had to help the woman or we wouldn't be good Christians.

Our friends implied we were selfish if we didn't come and do our part. From past programming, we believed that if the priest or enough people told us to do something that seemed good, then we would be wrong—and feel guilty—if we didn't do it.

When we listen to the voice of the superego and fail to make our own decisions, we take a shortcut. Like Adam and Eve, like the prodigal son, like Pilate, our efforts leave us feeling uncertain and unfulfilled.

What are some of the "you shoulds" in your life?

____

____

____

____

Making Your Own Moral Decisions

So, how do we make decisions that are not based on the opinions of others? Richard Gula identifies three parts of the moral conscience that operate in mature decision-making. The first part is our fundamental sense of responsibility. The second part is our search for what is right. We rely on sources of moral wisdom like Jesus' life and parables, other Scriptures, theologians, our own personal experiences, the experiences of family and friends, official teachings of the Church, and stories, actions, and traditions of our entire community.

The third part of our moral conscience is the part that leads us to act, the concrete judgment of what we must do. We recognize that the choice is ours and that we must be true to ourselves.

The process of making sound and mature moral decisions combines our fundamental sense of responsibility and our search for what is right; then, in the light of our own individual circumstances, we come to a decision. We then do what we believe is right and avoid what we believe is wrong.

In making our decision about working on the widow's home, Bill and I knew that we had an obligation at home that superceded working on the widow's house. But we didn't heed our own moral conscience. Our shortcut left us feeling greatly dissatisfied. We knew relief only when we took the long way around: explaining to Father and our friends that we simply did not believe the project was for us.

Gula summarizes the process of making moral choices by contrasting fear and love: "The superego—the voice of others—acts out of fear of losing love and the need to be accepted and approved. The moral conscience acts in love from the values we are committed to. To really learn to help other people, we must refuse to deal with the superego, listening to it as if it were our conscience and listen instead to the voice of our own moral conscience."

Personal Application

Write about a decision you must make now or of a past decision you want to reconsider. If no scene comes to mind, use the following:

> You love teaching in the parish religious-education program, but your spouse has been making cutting remarks about your absence on Sunday mornings. The director of the program is pushing you to commit to another year of teaching. You want to help, but you feel your main responsibility is to your spouse. If you don't teach, however, fifteen sixth-graders will not have a teacher next fall.

Determine two choices to this situation (or your own): one that is guided by your superego and one that is guided by your moral conscience.

Superego

When guided by your superego, your rules are someone else's. You feel you "should" do something in order to feel accepted and loved.

What authority influenced your decision?

____

____

____

____

What action did you decide to take?

____

____

____

____

Possible personal outcomes:

____

____

____

____

Moral Conscience

When guided by your moral conscience, you are led by the values you hold dear.

Identify your values by listing the things that influence your choices. (This is one of the most important things you can know about yourself.)

____

____

____

____

What action did you decide to take?

____

____

____

____

Possible personal outcomes:

____

____

____

____

Knowing what you know now about
listening to the voice of the superego
and taking a shortcut
versus
considering your own values
and taking the long way around,
read the following Scriptures again.

Genesis 3:1-5: What advice could you give to Eve?

____

____

Luke 15:11-18: What would you like to tell this lad before he starts out?

____

____

Matthew 27:19-26: Do you think Pilate would take your advice if you were able to offer it? Why or why not?

____

____

Wrap Up

Continue during the week: Explain the three parts of the conscience to a friend.

Especially for you: Nurture yourself; you are vitally important. Without you, there are a lot of people who will not be helped. Do something meaningful for yourself that your superego says is foolish.

Just for fun: Watch a TV drama or movie and decide if the main characters are acting from their superego or moral conscience. If you're doing this study in a group, watch the same movie and discuss it together. Suggested viewing: *Chariots of Fire.*

Journal: Write about a past choice that still touches a tender spot or still makes you shudder. Record an alternative choice based on what you've learned in this lesson.

Memorize: "I praise you, so wonderfully you made me; / wonderful are your works!" (Psalm 139:14).

Closing Prayer

Thank you, God, that I am created as a complex person. Through your grace, help me to know my real self.

Glory to the Father, and to the Son, and to the Holy Spirit; as it was in the beginning, is now, and will be for ever. Amen.

Lesson Two
Hospitality

For I was hungry and you gave me food...a stranger and you welcomed me.

Matthew 25:35

Beginning Prayer

Dear God, your Word says that sometimes when we welcome strangers, we welcome angels unaware. Let your Holy Spirit guide me into the gentle art of welcoming angels.

Glory to the Father, and to the Son, and to the Holy Spirit; as it was in the beginning, is now, and will be for ever. Amen.

The Lesson:
Learning to Welcome Others

The book was on hospitality, and I couldn't bear to finish it. It was too depressing. All that talk about dinner parties and decorations and serving pieces caused me to conclude that I was never going to be a hospitable person. I decided that when God handed out hospitality, I was taking care of children.

Later, I found out that hospitality is not about cutlery but about people. It's about welcoming others and letting them into my life. I learned that hospitality means creating a space in my life and welcoming others into it.

That is something I can do. I can create a space to make s'mores with my children or celebrate their birthdays or sit by their bedside at night. Hospitality is definitely within my reach.

That means I know a lot of hospitable people. There is Lois, who has a ready pot of coffee waiting when I come to her back door. There's Uncle Bill, who always had the time to talk with me when I was little, even though he was tired. There was Laurilee, who sat at the desk next to mine when we were young magazine editors. Not only did she make a place for me to reveal who I was but she shared her life, her dreams, and her heartaches with me.

Of course, hospitality includes the party-givers as well. We need them to host the faith-sharing groups and endless meetings. The world needs hospitality of every kind. People need to be welcomed, whether they are at the parish coffee hour or a home meeting or a hospital waiting room. Newcomers, in our mobile society, need to feel welcome on the job and in the neighborhood. While not all of us have the natural gift of hospitality, most of us can learn to practice it well enough so that those around us will know the warmth of feeling truly welcome.

While we were visiting Hawaii, my husband was rushed to a little island hospital, his heart fibrillating out of control. Far from home, I sat in that hospital waiting room and tried not to cry so noisily. A Hawaiian woman moved beside me and covered my hand with hers. I forget her words, but I will always remember the space she made in her life for me when I was so needy.

Read Matthew 25:34-40. Using this Scripture as a guide, what is one specific way you can create a space in your life to welcome others (or a particular person)?

____

____

Read Matthew 10:42 and reread Matthew 25:40. What do you hear Jesus saying to you about those times when you create a space in your life for others?

____

____

____

Sometimes it's hard to realize that even the smallest kindness done for someone is done for Jesus, yet that is the privilege we are offered.

The Bible gives us many different ideas about hospitality.

Read Romans 16:1-2. In what ways, do you think, did Phoebe create a space in her life and welcome others into it? Let your imagination soar.

____

____

Read 2 Kings 4:8-10. Elisha is a traveling prophet with no place to call his own in Shunem. What did the Shunammite woman offer him? Use your own words.

____

____

Read 2 Kings 4:11-37 and Hebrews 13:2. What parallel do you find in these two references?

____

____

Do you believe that anyone in the twentieth century can actually entertain an angel? ________ Really? ________

Look up the following Scriptures and note the giver and the hospitality gift. What attitude does the giver express?

Reference	Who	Gift	Attitude
Genesis 18:1-5	Abraham	place to wash place to rest a meal	________
Genesis 24:15-24	Rebekah	water	________
Exodus 2:16-20	Reuel	a meal	________
Acts 16:13-15	Lydia	place to sleep	________
Acts 16:25-34	Jailer	washed wounds a meal	________
Acts 28:1-2	People of Malta	a fire to warm them	________

What conclusions do you draw from these examples and attitudes?

____

____

Do you think that something small done willingly is more valuable than something large done unwillingly? Explain your response.

____

____

Sometimes it's tempting to think that what you have to give is so small no one could use it. Maybe your living space is tiny or your food budget is meager or your time is limited or you find talking with people difficult. Yet, no gift is insignificant.

Read Luke 9:10-17. What was the disciples' concern?

____

____

____

How many were in the crowd? Remember that only the men were counted, so make an estimate of how many women and children were there, too. _________ What food was brought to Jesus?

____

Did Jesus scorn five loaves and two fish? Did he say, "This is totally inadequate"? Not at all. He blessed what little there was—and fed everyone there. What does this say about the "size" of your hospitality gift?

____

____

____

What does this say about hospitality in the name of Jesus?

____

____

____

Ministry Circle

The Ministry Circle below consists of three circles. The dot in the center circle is you. The "H" stands for home; the "C" stands for community; the "G" stands for global.

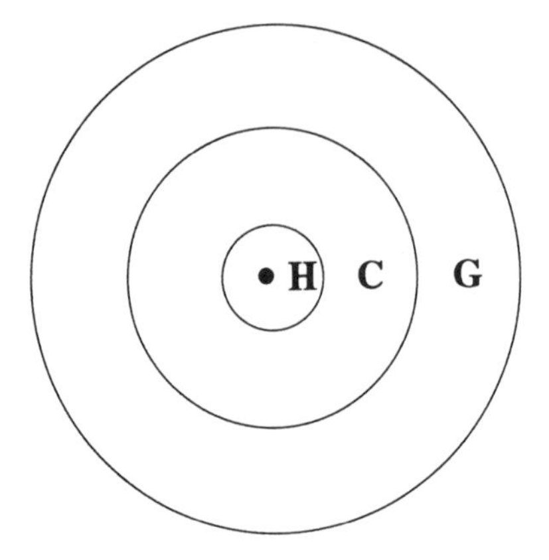

Obviously, your position in the Ministry Circle shows the direct, immediate, and powerful influence you have on the people in your home circle. Your community influence is important but further from the center where your impact is the strongest. You will have even less influence in the global circle that, although it is important, is on the periphery of your time and talents.

You can identify who most needs what you have to give by defining the people in your inner and outer circles. We will refer to these lists in future lessons, so think through the following exercise with deliberate care.

On the next page, list the names of the people who share your home circle (such as spouse, children, parents, grandchildren, grandparents, roommate, religious community, close neighbors, friends at work). The persons in your home circle may not actually live with you, but they are in the home of your heart.

Next, define the people in your community circle (such as the people in your place of work, neighborhood, parish, PTA, classroom, Bible study, prayer group, local political party, volunteer projects, aerobics group).

Who constitutes your global circle? Perhaps a missionary, a child in an Indian orphanage, a seminarian, a distant relative, a native priest? Sometimes your global circle may include populations suffering from natural disasters or the ravages of war.

The people who comprise my home circle are:

____________________ ____________________

____________________ ____________________

____________________ ____________________

____________________ ____________________

____________________ ____________________

____________________ ____________________

The people who comprise my community circle are:

____________________ ____________________

____________________ ____________________

____________________ ____________________

The people who comprise my global circle are:

____________________ ____________________

____________________ ____________________

____________________ ____________________

Personal Application

What kind of hospitality do you offer those in your home circle each day or week? Check the chart about hospitality gifts and attitudes on page 24 for some starting ideas.

____

____

____

____

Look over the gifts you just listed and ask yourself, *Is my giving influenced by my values or do the commands of my superego tell me what I have to do?* Perhaps it would help to compare your attitude with the attitudes of the biblical people we've just read about. A begrudging attitude probably is a good sign that you are working with the "I should" motive. Put a "V" (values) or an "S" (superego) beside each hospitality gift you listed above.

Take heart! Don't feel bad if you find you are giving with a begrudging heart. That happens to all of us when we get over-burdened with the cares of others. A begrudging heart simply means it's time to stop, take stock, and make some changes.

Who are the people you love and care for most?

____________________ ____________________

____________________ ____________________

How do you or could you make a space for them and welcome them into it?

____

____

Is there anything you want to change about the space you make for others in your life?

___

___

___

Hospitality also allows others to give to you. What do you allow or could you allow others in your home circle to give to you? If you hate to accept anything from someone else, give special thought to this question. Letting someone share your need is a way of helping them.

___

___

___

Now list the hospitality you offer in your community circle and ask yourself why you do what you do for these people.

___

___

___

Place a "V" (values) or an "S" (superego) by each hospitality gift you offer. Is there anything you want to stop doing? Circle it.

What do you allow the people in your community to give back to you?

___

___

How can you focus your gift of welcoming others so it can do the most good? This is a real "think-it-through" question. There is only so much of you and so many of them.

____

____

____

____

Who in your global circle needs a drink of cool water from you in Jesus' name? Remember: You are just a dot in a big circle. You have responsibilities at home and in the community. You want to reach out from your value system, not from the "I should" voice. Stop and pray: "Lord, how can I be hospitable to someone I cannot see or touch?" (Giving money is not a suitable answer here because hospitality implies welcoming someone into your life.)

A phone call that shares something of the real you and invites return sharing or maybe a warm letter to someone overseas comes to my mind. What comes to yours?

____

____

____

____

Summary: Making a space for someone in your life and welcoming him or her into it are gifts only you can give. When you welcome others, you welcome Jesus.

Wrap Up

Continue during the week: Explain your Ministry Circle to a good friend.

Gift Assessment Chart: In your current situation, what is the best way you can exercise the gift of hospitality?

____

____

Copy this onto the Gift Assessment Chart on page 124. If you think this will bring healing to yourself or others, circle it.

Especially for you: Allow yourself to be a guest. Who is the most welcoming person you know? Invite yourself for an evening and let yourself be cared for.

Just for fun: Invite your family or some friends for a backward meal: ice cream first, carrot sticks last. Oh, and wear your shirt backward, too.

Journal: Write about a time when you did not feel welcomed into someone else's space.

Memorize: "For I was hungry and you gave me food, I was thirsty and you gave me drink, a stranger and you welcomed me" (Matthew 25:35).

Closing Prayer

Dear God, please give me the grace I need to make others feel welcomed.

Glory to the Father, and to the Son, and to the Holy Spirit; as it was in the beginning, is now, and will be for ever. Amen.

Lesson Three
Encouragement

Jesus came and touched them, saying, "Rise, and do not be afraid."

Matthew 17:7

Beginning Prayer

Dear God, the meaning of encouragement is to come alongside someone and help him or her. Through your Holy Spirit, show me how to be this kind of person.

Glory to the Father, and to the Son, and to the Holy Spirit; as it was in the beginning, is now, and will be for ever. Amen.

The Lesson:
Walking Alongside Others

In my large extended family, I am the "mother frog." But in the world of national broadcasting, I had become a quivering tadpole.

When I was invited to be a guest on a national talk show, I accepted with pleasure. On the day of the show, however, I awakened in the hotel room with a cloud of doom hanging low. By the time I got to the studio, my knees were mush. In the small room outside the program set, with ten minutes until air-time, I was on the verge of tears. I couldn't do it; I couldn't face those cameras and a zillion viewers and say anything coherent, let alone helpful.

Sitting in the same room was one of the coguests, Al Kaska, the man who composed the music for "Pete's Dragon." He tried small talk, and I answered with stutters. "Are you afraid?" he asked.

I nodded, admitting to it.

He crossed the room, sat beside me on the sofa, picked up my hand, and held it in both of his. "You don't have to be afraid. God is with you. He's promised never to leave you, and he won't let you down now." Al stayed there beside me until we were called. Giving my hand a squeeze, he said, "Go on now, you can do it." And I did.

That was encouragement!

*

David is five years old. He sits beside his mother on the back steps and confides to her the sadness in his heart. "I've been thinking about something. I just figured out that I'm never going to be as good as Billy. He can run faster and count higher and do everything better. When I get to be seven like he is and can do everything as good as he can, he'll still be able to do it better." He puts his head in his mother's lap.

She remains silent for a while, because she hears the heart's cry of her small son. Then she has an idea. "David, I know what we're going to do. I'm going to teach you to swim. And you are going to learn to swim so well that you will always, always be the best swimmer in this whole family."

That's encouragement!

*

In our county jail for men, there are two rival factions. During Wednesday night Bible study, however, these two factions draw somewhat of a truce—while clinging to opposite sides of the room.

One night, halfway through the study, a large man interrupted and stood to his feet. "I hafta say something," he blurted. "I gotta get off the street. I gotta get out of gangs. I gotta get off drugs." Then he slumped back into his seat.

Across the room, a very small man stood up. All eyes were on him as he walked toward the big man. The small guy stopped in front of the big guy's chair, knelt down, and reached to put his hand on the big guy's heart.

The leader held his breath; "Big Guy" could knock the little one for a loop. The little guy spoke. "I got off the streets. I got out of gangs. I got off of drugs. *El Señor* (the Lord) helped me, and *el Señor* will help you, too."

That's encouragement to the heart!

*

At last, the Israelites had escaped from Pharaoh's tyranny and were safe on the banks of the Red Sea. What a relief! Suddenly, in a dark cloud of dust, they could see Pharaoh's soldiers hot in pursuit. "Oh, no," they gasped. All their struggles for freedom were crushed. Women screamed. Babies cried. Children cowered. Men feared. Not even Moses could save them now.

True it was, but Moses didn't have to save them from Pharaoh.

Read Exodus 14:13-14. Moses encouraged the Israelites to trust God. Remember, this was a great throng of people. Imagine the men closest at hand hearing Moses' strong encouragement and passing it on to others. They passed it on down the line until it eventually reached the women and children.

What happened next is still exciting history. The Israelites did not disperse madly and fall into the hands of the enemy. Encouraged, they…but don't let me tell you. Read this amazing epic yourself (Exodus 14:15-31).

*

In Capernaum, a man lay paralyzed: out of work, out of the mainstream, out of hope. They told him that there was a man, a holy teacher, who might help him, but how was he to get to the holy man? What's more, how would he face the holy man when his own sins weighed on him so heavily?

His friends came to his rescue. They picked up his mat, carried it past the crowds, and climbed to the rooftop with it. From there, they lowered the man and his mat before the holy teacher.

Read Luke 5:20. What were Jesus' encouraging words?

___

How do you think the paralyzed man felt?

___

How would you feel?

___

After this encouragement, Jesus had more good news.

Read verses 24-25. Note here how this man's life was changed.

___

___

Now go back to verse 20. What did Jesus see in the friends of the paralyzed man?

___

Knowing this about these men, write down the encouraging words they must have offered their friend as they carried him along on his mat.

___

___

Think of someone you know who is hurting. What words or deeds might encourage him or her?

___

___

___

Encouraging people can alter lives. For instance, in Jericho there lived a man who grew rich cheating his countrymen. I think he might have wanted to stop and that his conscience bothered him, but we don't know this for sure. We do know that he scrambled up a tree for a better view when he heard Jesus was coming. Jesus, walking along the dusty road and people thronging him, looked up.

Read Luke 19:1-5. What words did Jesus say to the man who swindled his own people?

___

What disparaging words did Jesus *not* say? (Use your imagination. I thought of "You jerk!")

___

What would you call the words of Jesus?

___

I call them encouraging. What would you call the words you've written that Jesus did not say?

____

Yes, I thought they were discouraging and defeating and devaluing.

Read Luke 19:8-9. In one word, what happened to Zac?

____

What did Zac do when Jesus encouraged him?

____

*

Up, up the steep mountainside they went. Jesus, Peter, John, and James. Suddenly, before their eyes, Jesus changed in appearance. Who did they meet? Ghosts?

Read Matthew 17:1-5. What happened on the mountain?

____

____

Read verse 6. What did those three tough fishermen do?

____

Read verse 7. Body language experts tell us that our actual words make up only ten percent of our communication. Body action and tone of voice supply the rest. With this in mind, how might Jesus have looked and sounded when he said, "Don't be afraid"?

____

____

Read John 8:3-5. In your own words, describe the circumstances.

____

____

____

How, do you think, did the woman feel at this point?

____

____

Read verses 9-11. What were the loving and encouraging words of Jesus?

____

____

How, do you think, did the woman feel at hearing such words?

____

____

Read Matthew 26:33, 69-75. Here is another person in desperate need of encouragement. What kind of a mess was Peter in?

____

____

____

Try to describe Peter's pain (v. 75).

____

____

Read John 21:15-19. Describe how Jesus might have looked when he said, "Follow me."

____

What do you think Peter felt after the healing words that Jesus forgave all?

____

One of the words I thought of was *valued.*

Personal Application

Encouraging people causes them to feel valued. Look at how Zacchaeus changed when he learned that Jesus valued him enough to come to his house.

Review the names you listed in your home circle on page 27. Do you value the people in your home circle? Do you value them enough? Do you look at them and say, "Aren't they incredible?" or do you look at them and think, *What's going to happen next?*

Your values come out in your words. If someone shows you an art project that is still a little raw, can you think of three good things to say to encourage the budding artist? If someone shares with you a plan or a goal and you know from hard experience that the plan needs a lot of refining before it works, can you still find three words of encouragement? In almost every case, people bring us their ideas not for advice but for encouragement.

Who in your home circle is most in need of encouragement?

____

How valued do you think this person feels?

____

Name three things that might cause this person to feel discouraged.

____

____

____

Name three ways you could encourage this person.

____

____

____

Sometimes we don't value the people around us enough because the voices of our superegos tell us they don't live up to the hopes and dreams of past authority figures in our lives. Ask yourself, *What are my real values regarding the people in my home circle?* Perhaps you've heard past voices of authority saying that you or someone else should be a lot better athlete or handle money more carefully or get better grades. These past voices may cause you to devalue your own present talents or the gifts of others.

What are past voices of authority saying to you about the people in your home circle?

____

____

What are your own values?

____

____

Let's practice a scenario: Your daughter comes home with one B and four Cs on her report card. People in your past demanded far better grades from you, so you know all the discouraging words that could be said. What encouraging words will you say to your daughter instead?

____

____

____

____

Will your words make your daughter feel valued or devalued?

*

Your son doesn't survive the basketball cuts. This is a great disappointment to you. In the back of your mind, you hear your own father's belittling voice when you didn't make the team. What encouraging words will you say to your son?

____

____

What devaluing words will you choose not to say?

____

____

*

Someone in your home circle is in a car accident. What do you say?

____

____

How valued will he or she feel after you have said this?

____

____

List the names of the people in your home circle and write an encouraging word that comes right from your heart. Let your encouragement show how much you value him or her.

Person	Encouraging words

Review the names you listed in your community circle on page 27. Do you value the people in your community circle? Do you value them enough?

A coworker shows you a picture of his "catch": a twenty-one-pound salmon. Although it may look as though he is boasting, he really wants you to give value to what he values. Even though you may have caught a fifty-pound tuna at one time, what encouraging thing could you say to this guy?

___

___

What discouraging comments come to your mind?

___

___

How will this person feel the rest of the day after your encouraging comment? ___

after your discouraging comment? ___

The following list identifies signals people give us when they are in need of encouragement:

extreme shyness	talkativeness
self-belittlement	exaggerated behavior
blaming others	dishonest excuses
denial of anger	denial of pain

List the names of people in your community circle who might be needing the strength and help of your encouraging words. What encouraging words can you offer each of these people?

Person	**Encouraging words**
___	___
___	___
___	___

Review the names you listed in your global circle on page 27. Do you value the people in your global circle? Do you value them enough?

Which of these persons could you encourage with a letter? I thought of writing an encouraging note to Pope John Paul II. Who did you come up with?

Summary: There's hardly a person who doesn't want to be valued. Your encouragement could alter the way people feel about themselves; your encouragement can alter people's lives.

Wrap Up

Continue during the week: Tell a friend the effects of the encouraging words you gave to someone else.

Gift Assessment Chart: In your current situation, what is the best way you can exercise the gift of encouragement?

Copy this onto the Gift Assessment Chart on page 124. If you think this will bring healing to yourself or others, circle it.

Especially for you: Sit down with an adult you can honestly trust and say, "I am in need of some encouragement. Please tell me three ways I am valued by you."

Just for fun: Put a treat in the top dresser drawer of everyone in your home circle.

Journal: Write about how valuable you are to this world. (Think about the film *It's a Wonderful Life* in which James Stewart is shown the empty spots that would have been in his town and family if he'd never been born.) Encourage yourself.

Memorize: "Jesus came and touched them, saying, 'Rise, and do not be afraid' " (Matthew 17:7).

Closing Prayer

Dear God, thank you for loving me so much that you sent Jesus into the world for me. Thank you that I am that valuable. Through your Holy Spirit, help me to encourage and value others.

Glory to the Father, and to the Son, and to the Holy Spirit; as it was in the beginning, is now, and will be for ever. Amen.

Lesson Four
Giving

"Give and gifts will be given to you...For the measure with which you measure will in return be measured out to you."

Luke 6:38

Beginning Prayer

Dear God, you have given so much to me. Please let your Holy Spirit guide me onto the pathways of giving.

Glory to the Father, and to the Son, and to the Holy Spirit; as it was in the beginning, is now, and will be for ever. Amen.

The Lesson: God Requires Us to Give to Others and Blesses Our Efforts

This is a story of generosity on my part, but I tell it only to show the greater generosity on the part of God.

Because we're a big family, we often receive boxes of used clothing. I go through the boxes and sort out what we can use; what we can't use (or what needs ironing), I take to a center that will distribute it to the poor.

I was sorting through one of these boxes one day, and as a last-minute thought, I added an old, faded bath towel from my laundry basket.

When I arrived at the distribution center with my boxes and that bath towel on top, a woman jumped to her feet and exclaimed, "Oh, if I could have that towel I'd be so happy. I'd take me a bath, and then I'd rub and rub and rub." For the first time, I realized that there are people who don't have the simple necessity of towels.

I'm not sure why I did what I did, but I returned home and brought back to the woman my two best towels. They were pink with flamingos on them. We never used them as bath towels; rather, I kept them on the towel racks to hide the ghastly rust that was corroding the old-fashioned metal tile on the bathroom walls.

About a week after this incident, Bill and I were driving through town. Suddenly he pulled into a parking spot in front of a tile store. "What are you doing?" I asked.

"I don't know," he replied, "I just felt like I should stop."

We went inside and right by the door were five boxes of beige tile on sale for almost nothing. As we paid for them, the salesclerk shook his head and said, "I don't know why we're selling these at this price."

There's even more to the story. Unless Bill has someone to work with him, he is totally unhandy around the house. (He gave me permission to share that fact.) But he pried the ugly, rusted metal tile away from the bathroom walls, prepared the walls, and put up the new tile—by himself. Today, our bathroom is resplendent. I never regretted giving the pink flamingo towels to the lady who had none.

Was this giving and receiving a coincidence? I don't think so. I've heard similar stories from others.

Read Luke 6:38. What happens when you give?

____

How much? ____________________________________

What kind of measuring cup will the Giver use?

___

God is the giver. If we use a person-sized cup to measure our gifts, how big might a God-sized cup be?

___

What does this tell you about the way God views our giving?

___

___

Read Luke 14:12-14. There's nothing wrong with giving gifts to our friends and family members. But there's another dimension to giving. Who else are we to give to?

___

Why? ___

Why, do you think, is it important to give to others?

___

___

*

When Dave arrived to pick up his son, he stayed a few extra minutes for a cup of coffee. As we visited, he shared his story. He'd lost his job, and his wife had left him with five children to care for and a debt of over $5,000. He had $14.50 left to his name. "I have no idea where to turn or what to do."

I asked if he'd ever heard of tithing. "No, what's that?"

Read Malachi 3:10. (Malachi is the last book in the Old Testament.)

A tithe is ten percent of your income. In biblical days, it was ten percent of all harvested crops and every tenth new animal. What does the above Scripture passage say we are to do with this tithe?

____

____

What does God promise? He will __________ and __________ so much ______________ that you will not have ____________ to take it in.

"Dave," I told him that morning as we read the passages from Malachi, "I think all you've got going for you right now is God's promise. Will you give a tenth of your $14.50 to God and trust in him?"

The next morning at Mass, Dave dropped one tenth of his money, $1.45, in the offering. It was a generous sum for a man with five children to feed.

Before the week was out, two significant things happened. The credit union that held the $5,000 debt called to say that it was totally forgiven. The business firm that had laid Dave off called and offered him his job back at a higher salary.

Read Malachi 3:11. What are two other promises God gives to those who, like Dave, will tithe? God will prevent _________ from ____________________. The ________________ in your fields will not ____________.

How would you put these promises in today's language?

____

____

One thing I know for sure: people who tithe don't have nearly as many unexpected, budget-destroying expenses.

Read the following Scriptures and summarize their messages about the personal results of giving to God.

Proverbs 11:25 ______________________________

____

____

Isaiah 58:10 ______________________________

____

____

2 Corinthians 9:6 ______________________________

____

____

*

My friend Melody was visiting a large city where there are underground pedestrian walkways. In a passage one morning, she came upon a person so unkempt that she couldn't tell if the person was a man or woman. Like the rest of the crowd, she turned her eyes away, not wanting to look at the pitiful and filthy nest the person slept in.

But Melody felt unsettled as she walked to the end of the passage and up the stairs to the street. She wanted to respond to the person in the passage but didn't know how. Having just a little bit of money and not knowing what else she could do, she continued walking.

As Melody past a McDonald's, she knew what to do. She bought a cup of coffee and a hamburger and hurried back to the underground walkway. She offered the coffee and sandwich to the person. "Hi, I've brought breakfast."

"For me?" The ragged form sat up on one elbow. "God bless ye." The voice, although hoarse, was surely that of a woman. "I can't take all of this. Here, I'll share it with ye."

Melody was touched by such unparalleled generosity. "No, it's all for you." She left the woman with the meager meal and hurried on her way, but she said that something like joy bells rang within her heart.

Read Acts of the Apostles 20:35. What does Jesus say about giving?

____

____

Read Mark 12:41-44 and 2 Corinthians 8:1-4. With the theme of these passages in mind, comment on the joy bells that rang for Melody.

____

____

What kind of giving is modeled for us in this Scripture?

____

____

Comment on the gladness and generousness of Melody's gift.

____

____

Giving to others in today's society is not necessarily a Christian act. Look at all the people who contribute gladly and generously to the United Appeal or to the Arts or to humanitarian causes.

"Done unto God": this is the distinguishing characteristic of Christian giving. It is to God that we bring our Sunday offering, and it is unto God that we send money to the missions. It is unto God that we give to our brothers and sisters in need. It is unto God that we give in our home, community, and global circles. When we give our gift unto God, it is God who reaps benefits upon us. For when we give unto him as he has asked, he is never outdone in generosity to us.

Personal Application

This is where we face the superego head on. Its commands and all those past voices of authority hammer at us to give here and here and here until the joy of giving evades us.

How can you give generously and gladly to those in your home circle so that your giving is done cheerfully? Review the list of names in your home circle on page 27. Which of the following gifts have been part of your giving to these people?

_____ Money gifts of rent or mortgage
_____ Money gifts of groceries
_____ Money expense of holidays
_____ Money expense of transportation
_____ Money expense of clothing
_____ Time expense of cooking
_____ Time expense of cleaning
_____ Time expense of repairing
_____ Time expense of driving
_____ Time expense of budgeting

What can you do or stop doing to make gladness and generosity characteristics of your giving? Start by answering the following.

What does your superego say "you must" give to your family?

___

___

___

What are your values? What do you really want to give?

___

___

___

In my own life, I found more time for the people in my home circle by eliminating a lot of housework—housework I did simply because past voices told me to do it. For example, my mother said that sheets must be changed weekly, so I changed every sheet in the house every week. I knew I "should." Then one week I didn't change the sheets. Do you know what happened? Nothing. So I didn't change them for another week. This time something did happen. I broke forever with a rule I never made in the first place. In one small way, I had more time for what really mattered.

Gladly and generously, write suggestions that will help you give what you want to give in your home circle.

___

___

___

___

Review the list of names in your community circle on page 27. It is in your community circle that you consider the words from Malachi 3:10: "Bring the whole tithe into the storehouse." In biblical days, ten percent of the crops were brought to the priests who had no land of their own on which to support themselves. From that, we reason that the ten percent we give from our salaries today goes to provide for those who need it: the parish, the missions, the diocese, the poor.

A tithe is a generous amount to give away, especially when given gladly. But, as we have seen, God honors generosity. "Try me and see," God says.

How much would be ten percent for you? ________________

Where might you give it?

____

____

____

____

If your spouse or community cannot be persuaded to give ten percent, what can you gladly and generously "bring to the storehouse" from your own resources? Remember the widow's mite. God always looks at our heart in this matter of giving.

________________ ________________

________________ ________________

________________ ________________

Review the list of names in your global circle on page 27. How can you reach out to these people with gladness and generosity?

I thought of supporting a child or parish in Africa. What idea did you come up with?

____

____

Summary: God asks us to give and then he honors our giving. He asks that this giving be done generously and gladly.

Wrap Up

Continue during the week: Share with a friend the changes you will make in your home circle that will gladden your giving.

Gift Assessment Chart: In your current situation, what is the best way you can exercise the gift of giving?

____

____

Copy this onto the Gift Assessment Chart on page 124. If you think this will bring healing to yourself or others, circle it.

Especially for you: You and Jesus together are off to the mall or hobby shop or deli. This is going to be a good time.

Just for fun: Wear a paper hat. Don't tell anyone why.

Journal: Was someone ever stingy with you? Was someone ever generous with you? Write about how both experiences felt.

Memorize: "Give and gifts will be given to you....For the measure with which you measure will in return be measured out to you" (Luke 6:38).

Closing Prayer

Dear God, I want to be generous with you. Please give me the grace to be a cheerful giver.

Glory to the Father, and to the Son, and to the Holy Spirit; as it was in the beginning, is now, and will be for ever. Amen.

Lesson Five
Teaching

We recite them to the next generation...
that they too might put their trust in God....
Psalm 78:4, 7

Beginning Prayer

Dear God, out of the thousands of ways there are to teach others, please help me, through your Holy Spirit, to be the kind of teacher you want me to be.

Glory to the Father, and to the Son, and to the Holy Spirit; as it was in the beginning, is now, and will be for ever. Amen.

The Lesson:
Every One of Us Can Be a Teacher

Paul was only a toddler when his father began to teach him. He couldn't even comprehend the Bible stories his father would read him.

His father would sit on the edge of Paul's bed and teach him prayers. His father acted out the parables of Jesus so Paul could better understand them.

By the time Paul was barely five years old, he had grasped a theological principle. "Papa, I've been thinking. The dog and the cat don't know that God made them, but we do."

On a long ago day, Paul died in an accident. But his father knew that when Paul met Jesus face to face, they were already friends.

*

It was thirty-five years ago, and I was teaching my first religious-education class. I had a carefully prepared lesson—or so I thought. But when I got to the end of it, I still had fifteen minutes to fill before the children would be dismissed. I had no tricks of a teacher to fall back on and no idea how to fill that time. I was panicky because I'd used up every bit of resource available, and eight ninth-grade girls were looking at me to see what was coming next.

Grabbing at anything, I began to tell them how I prayed the rosary using the little book that was in the back of church. I told them how real the mysteries were because of what the little book said. I spoke from my experience and from my heart. As I finished, the hands of the clock reached their slow journey to nine o'clock and the class was over.

The next week the girls said, "We went to the back of church, and the little book on saying the rosary wasn't there. Could you find some for us?"

I can still remember the feeling of that moment. *I taught them something. They heard it. They remembered it. They acted on it.* At that moment, I learned what it means to be a teacher. I understood: one teaches because one has something to give that will make a difference in someone else's life.

*

The man took his six children to the zoo. The price for children was one dollar for each child over five years of age; his youngest was six. Having very little money, the father glanced down on his six-year-old: *I bet I can get him in for free.* The ticket seller said, "How many children over five?"

The man looked down at the faces of all his children before he answered. "Six," he said.

It cost this father an extra dollar to be honest, but the lesson he taught was priceless.

*

Teaching doesn't always mean schoolrooms, chalkboards, desks, or degrees in education. Let's look at Jesus' classroom. Read the following Scripture passages and note where Jesus taught:

Matthew 5:1-2 ______________________________

Mark 4:1 ______________________________

John 7:14 ______________________________

Where do these Scriptures suggest that your classroom may be?

____

____

Read Deuteronomy 6:4-6. What is it we (Israel) must hear?

(v. 4)______________________________

____

What are we commanded?

(v. 5)______________________________

____

(Also read Deuteronomy 5:6-21.)

Where are we to hold or carry these commands?

(v. 6)______________________________

____

Read Deuteronomy 6:7-9. What are we to do with these commands that are finding a place in our heart?

____

____

____

Read Deuteronomy 6:12. Why must we talk and talk and talk so much about what God wants of us?

____

____

Following God's ways ensures that we do not forget him. Teaching others to follow in his ways ensures that they will not forget him either.

Read Psalm 78:1-5, 7-8. What are the children and the next generation to be taught?

(v. 4)____

____

and (v. 5)______________________________________

____

What will be the result?

(v. 7)____

____

and (v. 8)______________________________________

____

In this Psalm, what makes the difference between praising the Lord and becoming unfaithful to him?

____

____

You may say, "But I've taught my children and look at the mess their lives are in." I remember feeling terrible pain when one of our sons walked away from our teaching with the words "I don't need God." I wish I'd known then how really faithful God is, for it would have saved so much heartache. In time, the phone rang and this son said, "We're getting married at St. John's in three weeks. Can you come?" Then he added, "Mom, we really do need God."

Teaching from your heart to the hearts of others—over and over—makes the difference. Much of Jesus' teaching already lives in your heart, because you've experienced it firsthand.

Read the following Scripture passages and note the lesson each one teaches:

Matthew 5:11 ________________________________

Matthew 5:24 ________________________________

Matthew 5:44 ________________________________

Matthew 6:6 ________________________________

Matthew 6:14 ________________________________

Matthew 6:25 ________________________________

Matthew 7:1 ________________________________

Matthew 7:7 ________________________________

Which of the previous Scripture lessons, or any of the teaching Scriptures (Matthew 5, 6, 7), lives in your heart?

____

____

____

What would happen if you taught your children, grandchildren, neighbor children, or parish children those things of God that live in your heart? Scripture offers answers to this question.

Read Ephesians 4:12-13. What happens when you teach others about Christ?

____

____

____

Read Ephesians 4:14. What other good reasons are offered?

____

____

How does good teaching affect a person's life?

____

____

____

Personal Application

In your home, community, and global circles, there are many opportunities for you to teach. Review the list of names in your home circle on page 27. What do you consider the most important truths that you could teach in your home circle?

____

____

____

What is the difference between teaching from the Scripture in your heart and teaching from the inner commands of the superego?

____

____

____

____

Teaching can't be left to chance, so let's make a plan for getting started.

At bedtime, I can teach about

____

____

At mealtime, I can teach about

____

____

On Sunday night, I can teach about

____

____

While rubbing someone's shoulders, I can teach about

____

____

Add your ideas about a time to teach, a place to teach, and what to teach.

____

____

____

Review the list of names in your community circle on page 27. What plans can you make for teaching God's commands to teenagers or adults, some of who may not want to hear anything about God. To be genuine, any plan must come from your heart (your values) and not the superego.

I could set a good example like

____

I could recommend reading material like

____

I could say things like

____

I could invite others to go to

____

Your parish religious-education program may be a good place to help as a teacher or an aide. Parish teaching has lasting value. Remember: it's important to teach. It's something that lasts into the next generation. It changes the direction of lives. But your teaching has to be right for your situation. It doesn't have to be today or next week. You will be the best teacher when you are ready for the job.

Look ahead to the next several years of your life. When could you begin to volunteer or get involved?

____

____

Look at the names listed in your global circle on page 27. How can you teach these people? I mailed *The Hiding Place,* the highly adventurous story of a Christian woman who hid Jews during World War II, to an interested Jewish woman I met on a plane. That's what comes to my mind. What comes to yours?

____

____

____

> *Summary:* When we teach the ways of God from the classrooms of our lives, we help those we teach to walk in his ways. They will be strengthened and grow in maturity.

Wrap Up

Continue during the week: Go to your Catholic or Christian bookstore and pick out a teaching tool that you can use for teaching someone in your life. Show your purchase to a friend and explain how you are going to use it.

Gift Assessment Chart: In your current situation, how can you best exercise the gift of teaching?

____

____

Copy this onto the Gift Assessment Chart on page 125. If you think this will bring healing to yourself or others, circle it.

Especially for you: Let this be the week you read that book or do that special thing you've been putting off for so long.

Just for fun: Watch *The Hiding Place* on video.

Journal: Write about a teacher you remember. Write about the negative or positive influences he or she had on your life.

Memorize: "We recite them to the next generation… / that they too might put their trust in God…" (Psalm 78:4, 7).

Closing Prayer

Dear God, I thank you for the teachers in my life who have led me closer to you. I ask you for the grace I need to be a teacher to others.

Glory to the Father, and to the Son, and to the Holy Spirit; as it was in the beginning, is now, and will be for ever. Amen.

Lesson Six
Listening

Comfort, give comfort to my people,
says your God.

Isaiah 40:1

Beginning Prayer

Dear God, it feels so good when someone listens to me; please send your Holy Spirit to teach me how to listen to others with my heart.

Glory to the Father, and to the Son, and to the Holy Spirit; as it was in the beginning, is now, and will be for ever. Amen.

The Lesson:
Listening to Someone Else Can Bring Healing to Them

Dorie was eight years old when her stepfather began to sexually abuse her. "If you ever tell," he warned Dorie, "your mother will put you and your sister in an orphanage." Dorie kept the terrible secret locked within her, protecting herself and her little sister. When Dorie was twelve, she decided to tell her girlfriend. "My stepfather touches me here," she confided, pointing to her newly developed breasts. Dorie ached for her friend to understand so she could disclose the true picture, but her friend shouted, "He does not!" She ran off, leaving Dorie stunned. Her stepfather didn't need to warn her anymore about keeping quiet: there was no one in the world to tell.

When Dorie was thirteen, the abuse suddenly stopped—but life was not the same. Her memories were filled with shame and pain. She felt dirty and unworthy of friendships. While the other girls giggled over notes from boys and snickered in sex-education classes, Dorie turned further away from their silly ignorance. She did not know the alarming statistics on childhood sexual abuse. She felt she was the only one it had ever happened to.

As an adult, depression dogged Dorie's days and nights. She went to a Christian conference on overcoming depression and came away furious. The conference was on self-esteem. Dorie wanted to scream. She didn't want another lecture or book on self-esteem; Dorie wanted someone in her life to care about what had happened.

Mustering her courage, Dorie finally talked about her experiences with some friends. Their messages were "Don't talk about it," "Don't be so angry," and "Why do you have to go on and on and on?" One lady wanted Dorie to pray with her to trust God. When Dorie didn't feel any better after the prayer, the woman was visibly upset. Everyone wanted Dorie to hurry up and get better.

After much loneliness and isolation, Dorie finally experienced a breakthrough. She met a woman who understood. "She let me talk. She didn't try to fix my problem. She listened and she cared. She helped me grieve for my greatest loss: my childhood."

Therapy followed. Out of her pain, Dorie organized a group of women who, like herself, were survivors of childhood sexual abuse. The group accepted the unspeakable acts that had happened, acknowledged one another's pain, allowed one another to be angry, and expressed their real feelings without fear that the others would run away.

This kind of listening and acceptance brought the self-acceptance Dorie needed to break away from her isolation, shame, and depression.

*

In the small community in which we lived, there were no professional services to help hurting women. That's why I, with only limited counseling experience, was asked to facilitate a group of wounded women. For five hours, I listened to some unbelievable stories. How could God's precious children have been treated so brutally?

In my heart, I committed myself to these women. Going to the group meetings became my highest "nonfamily" priority. The second time we met, they all told the same stories again. Once more, I listened. The most common refrain was "I've never told anyone…my husband doesn't know…my best friend doesn't even guess." Now, at last, it was getting told.

My role over the months was always the same: listener. I wanted to do more, but I only listened. I loved these women so much that their stories were never tiresome. In time, the cofacilitator and I noted that other issues were coming up, and we considered that a good sign. The past traumas were losing their power in the retelling and acceptance.

It was such a small gift in proportion to how much good it did. At the last meeting I attended before I moved, we gave one another a final hug. "You listened to us," they said, "and our lives will never be the same again."

*

Bill and I discovered on another level that someone who really listens can make a huge difference. After we read John Powell's book *Why Am I Afraid to Tell You Who I Am?* we decided to follow one of his suggestions to see what would happen.

Each of us was to talk on any subject we chose for half an hour. The other would listen and not interrupt except to clarify a point.

Half an hour turned out to be a long time. For me, the first ten minutes went fine, but after that, I had to draw deeper for what I wanted to say. As a result, I shared inner thoughts I'd never voiced before. It was exhilarating to be listened to for so long. When it was Bill's turn to speak for half an hour, he said, "What I have to say is only going to take a few minutes." Two hours later, he was still talking. In short, both the speaker and the listener grew to know themselves and each other in new ways.

*

One of the reasons we don't like to listen to others is that their pain often makes us uncomfortable. But Jesus models for us the importance of sharing another's pain.

Read John 11:17-36. What does Jesus do when he sees Mary weeping?

On the surface, Jesus' weeping doesn't seem to make any sense. Jesus knew Lazarus was going to come back from the dead before the end of the day. He knew Mary's and Martha's mourning would be turned to gladness. Logically, there was no cause for sorrow. Except! Mary's and Martha's sorrow was so great that it touched Jesus' heart.

Read Matthew 16:21-22. It's human nature to try to discourage people from sorrowful talk. What does Jesus tell Peter?

What does Peter reply?

____

What kind of response do you think Jesus might have wanted from Peter?

____

Jesus was God, and yet he still looked for understanding and comfort. Does that make sense to you? ________________

Explain. ______________________________________

____

____

Is there anyone you know who is so together that he or she doesn't need understanding and comfort?

____

Read Matthew 26:36-40. What was Jesus' pain?

____

What did he want from his friends?

____

Read Luke 22:42-45 and Mark 14:36-40. Put in your own words what Jesus was saying to his disciples from his heart.

____

____

Read John 12:1-8. Among his followers, Jesus made it clear that he would die (Matthew 20:18-19). Although many were in denial over this, one woman, Mary, listened clearly enough to understand. What did she do with burial perfume?

___

Judas complained about this. Put Jesus' reply in your own words.

___

___

Mary's action showed grief for her friend, and Jesus did not try to "make her feel good." He respected her sorrow. Do you think Mary's sorrow was comforting to Jesus? ___
Why or why not?

___

___

___

Read Romans 12:9-21. Here are some exhortations for Christians on how to live their commitments. The directives that concern us in this lesson are in verse 15. Write them here.

___

___

___

___

Many people rejoice or mourn with others by telling them their own stories of victory or sorrow. That may work occasionally but, overall, if someone begins to tell you their story, what is the best response you could give? For example, if I come to work with puffy eyes and say "My little dog I've had for seven years died last night," my sorrow is real. Even though you think people who cry over pets are weird, how would you mourn with me?

---

*

I remember telling a friend about a painful comment a close relative had made to me. My friend said, "I'm so sorry that she said that to you. That was mean." Unexpected tears came to my eyes over those understanding words. I needed the comfort they offered more than I realized. What's more, the hurtful words spoken by that relative never hurt again.

*

I stop by your desk and announce, "I hit my first home run last night." For me, it's a spectacular accomplishment. For you, it means nothing. How can you rejoice with me?

Or perhaps you've tried for years to hit a home run, with no success. How do you rejoice with my accomplishment?

Listening and affirming are powerful means for transforming people and relationships. The person who listens with love can virtually change the lives of others.

Personal Application

Review the list of names in your home circle on page 27. Who are the youngest people in your home circle?

A. ____________________ C. ____________________

B. ____________________ D. ____________________

What do they want you to hear them say?

A. ____

B. ____

C. ____

D. ____

What time of day are they most willing to talk?

A. ____________________ C. ____________________

B. ____________________ D. ____________________

What can you do if you are engrossed in a favorite TV program when they want to talk to you? On a scale of 1 to 10 (ten the highest), rate the importance of the TV program and the importance of listening.

The TV program ______________________________

Listening ______________________________

Psychologist Dr. James Dobson says that the average father listens to his child *three minutes a week.* That's surprising, and yet it's not. We are so busy that some things don't seem important enough to take up our time. One father, shocked by the above statistic, decided to take his children, one at a time, on successive Thursdays for ice cream and listening.

What can you do to find a time to listen to the youngest people in your home circle?

A. ____

B. ____

C. ____

D. ____

If there are adults or near-adults in your home circle, it's possible that:

- They don't want your advice.
- They don't want your commands about what they should do next.
- They don't want you to solve their problems.
- They just want you to listen.

You can do three things.

- You can play back a little of what they've said so they can decide if what they are saying makes sense.
- You can assure them they are not alone and that they are loved.
- If they are in pain (and that's likely), you can share the pain with them.

Who else in your home circle could use some listening?

__________________ __________________

__________________ __________________

__________________ __________________

There are key phrases that convey your willingness to listen. Here are a few suggestions. Add your own.

How did your test go?
How do you feel about what he said to you?
Can you tell me about it?

____

____

____

____

Who are the elderly persons in your home circle?

__________________ __________________

__________________ __________________

Have you heard all their stories? all their fears? all their troubles? If you listened all over again, knowing that listening is healing, what difference could it make to them?

____

____

____

____

What difference could it make to you?

____

____

____

Are there limits to listening? Is there a point when your listening crosses the line from wanting to listen because listening is one of your values, to listening because your superego tells you that you "should" do it or "have" to do it? Would it be better not to listen if you really don't care what the person is saying? How can you solve this dilemma in a way that's right for you?

____

____

____

____

Review the names you listed in your community circle on page 27. Are there any people who would benefit from meeting together in a group and sharing common past hurts in the context of love, listening, and acceptance?

____________________ ____________________

____________________ ____________________

Additional thoughts on this are:

____

On page 122 is a list of guidelines for getting such a group started. Many people have been helped by finding a safe place to uncover their hurts.

Perhaps your listening ministry will be one-on-one rather than in a group. Remember: you don't have to make anyone better. You only listen. Who in your community circle needs a listener?

____________________ ____________________

____________________ ____________________

____________________ ____________________

Review the list of names in your global circle on page 27. Do any of them need you to listen to them? People everywhere are looking for a listener. Some tell problems, many tell stories. The person next to you on the bus or plane may want to talk. What other opportunities come to mind?

____

____

____

____

> *Summary:* Sharing in the suffering of other people by listening to their stories is one of the surest ways of reaching out to others. All people, even Jesus while here on earth, have times when they need the comfort of a listener.

Wrap Up

Continue during the week: Tell a friend about someone you plan to listen to with special attention this week. Report the results back to your friend.

Gift Assessment Chart: In your current situation, how can you best exercise the gift of listening?

____

____

Copy this onto the Gift Assessment Chart on page 125. If you think this will bring healing to yourself or others, circle it.

Especially for you: Find someone who will exchange half-hours of listening with you. This could be a wonderful beginning for both of you.

Just for fun: Do something with water: wade in a lake; take a long, soapy bath; or sneak up on the kids with a water pistol.

Journal: Today, speak to the Listener. Write to God about a time of suffering in your life. Tell it all to God: everything. God won't tell you to get your act together. God always, always listens.

Memorize: "Comfort, give comfort to my people" (Isaiah 40:1).

Closing Prayer

Dear God, thank you for always hearing me. Please give me the grace I need so that my listening to others can bring healing.

Glory to the Father, and to the Son, and to the Holy Spirit; as it was in the beginning, is now, and will be for ever. Amen.

Lesson Seven
Leadership

Then I heard the voice of the Lord saying, "Whom shall I send? Who will go for us?" "Here I am," I said; "send me!"

Isaiah 6:8

Beginning Prayer

Dear God, through your Holy Spirit, show me what it means to be a leader.

Glory to the Father, and to the Son, and to the Holy Spirit; as it was in the beginning, is now, and will be for ever. Amen.

The Lesson:
Choices, Not Positions, Make Leaders

Kirk Barre was an ordinary family man who went off to work each day. Then one day he met Ada. Kirk hardly ever noticed women, but he noticed how pretty Ada was the day she came for the interview. He started stopping in her office for a chat each morning. At lunchtime, rather than shutting his office door, he kept it open—just in case Ada might need something. She often stopped by and pulled up a chair. What he liked best about her was that she was so cheery. It was uplifting to talk with her.

"Of course," Kirk said to himself, "there's nothing to our conversations; we're just friends."

But Kirk thought a great deal about Ada. He began to note things that he wanted to tell her; he began to look forward to seeing her at work each morning. For the first time in years, Kirk began to get haircuts before he needed them. When Christmas came, he wondered what he could get Ada for a gift.

Out shopping with his wife, he picked out three nice presents. "For the women at work," he explained. "It's expected."

His wife questioned him, "You only have two women working for you, Kirk."

"The other one's for Ada. She takes my messages sometimes." He tried to sound casual.

There was concern in his wife's voice. "But Ada doesn't work for you, Kirk, and I feel uncomfortable about you giving her a gift."

"There's no reason to be upset, Cathy."

"I think you should look at your motives."

Instead of leaving the gifts home for his wife to wrap as he ordinarily did, Kirk took them to work and hid them in his credenza. There they sat, their presence distracting him.

Then Kirk began to feel uneasy when he stopped in Ada's office—and that made him angry. After all, she was *just a friend.* At Mass, Kirk prayed about the whole unsettling situation and hoped for a solution.

The traditional day for office gift-giving was the day before the Christmas break began. Kirk placed the two for the women who worked for him on their desks and went back to his office and brooded. Deep inside, he knew what he had to do. He gave the third gift to the cleaning lady. As he did, he knew there would be no more morning chats and that he'd be keeping his office door shut at lunchtime.

The decision left Kirk with a deep sense of loss, but he would not go back on it. Of that he was certain.

By stopping something compromising before it got started, Kirk touched a lot of lives: Cathy's, their children's, Ada's, Ada's husband's, their children's, his friends', Ada's friends', the other employees'. Kirk Barre made the choice of a leader.

*

Auschwitz 1941: Six hundred tense prisoners formed ten lines. The silence was absolute. "The fugitive from Block 14 has not been found," barked the venomous Nazi guard. "You will pay."

"You and you and you," he pointed and commanded, "over there!" For one escaped prisoner, ten would be put to death, not a merciful shooting death but a lingering death by starvation. Ten naked men would be put into a freezing subterranean cell without food or water until all had died. The first to die would have it the easiest. The last to die...it was too ghastly to comprehend.

The tenth prisoner was picked: a young Jewish man whose wife had just given birth. "No, no, please not me," he sobbed and pleaded. "My wife, my babies." The SS guards ignored him.

Maximilian Kolbe stepped forward from the ranks. "Herr Commandant, I wish to make a request. I want to die in place of the prisoner." He pointed to the sobbing man. "I have no wife or children."

"Who are you?"

"A Catholic priest."

The other prisoners stared in disbelief. Each had been focusing totally on his own life, holding his breath against being chosen.

The deputy commander snapped. "Request granted." He kicked the young Jew away and ordered the priest to take his place. The priest was the last of the ten men to die. He lived fourteen agonizing prayer-filled days. Later, witnesses of that death camp were to say that Maximilian Kolbe did not die for just one man. His heroic gift convinced thousands of prisoners that the true world existed. His death, they said, was the salvation of thousands.

Maximilian Kolbe died the death of a leader.

*

Melody and her husband have four teenagers, which made for a busy household during the summer months. Then Melody's sister-in-law came with her four small children. Next, two nephews arrived from California to spend some time with Melody and her family while their parents "sorted things out." Altogether, there were thirteen people to keep track of, shop for, and cook for.

At first everyone chipped in, and it was enjoyable. But after a while, although her sister-in-law helped, most of the work fell on Melody. One sticky, hot afternoon with still two weeks of company to go, Melody felt like she couldn't go on. It was too hard. *I'm just going to run away,* she told herself. As she poured blackberries into the blender, she plotted her escape. She wouldn't just leave, she'd call the retreat house and schedule a ten-day retreat. Her leaving would be spiritual and civilized. *Let the rest of them take over for a while,* she reasoned. *It's only fair.*

Preoccupied, Melody turned on the blender without the lid. The mess was indescribable. She spent an hour cleaning up blackberry pulp. While she cleaned, she thought and prayed, and prayed and thought. As the last black-and-blue smudge was wiped away, Melody finalized her plan. She'd stay home, take care of the family, take care of her nephews, work beside her sister-in-law, and ask God for the grace to keep on for two more weeks. And she did.

Melody's choice—that no one ever knew about—touched all the people of her family. In her own small way, Melody was a leader.

*

The world needs men and women who will be leaders, people we can look up to, people who will make courageous choices and show us the way.

If you choose to reach out to others as a leader, you will touch the lives of everyone around you, which means you will touch the life of the whole Church.

Being a leader doesn't mean you have to be a priest, deacon, corporate executive, president of the parish council, or chairperson of a committee. It doesn't mean you have to be organized or efficient. Being a leader has to do with making personal choices for the good of all.

*

No one would have guessed the outcome, especially the brothers who sold him. He was seventeen, a kid, and in many ways a spoiled teenager. He was taken far from his family to another country and culture. There he became a slave. Joseph is one of history's best-loved leaders.

Read Genesis 37:17-29, 36. What country did Joseph end up in? What happened to him?

(v. 36) ____

____

Read Genesis 39:1-10. What was Joseph's famous choice?

____

____

Let's leave Joseph for a moment and look at another potential leader.

Read Genesis 2:8-20. Adam has a tremendous leadership position. Can you think of a modern job description for him?

____

____

I thought of "CEO for Worldwide Gardens, Inc." Who did you think of?

____

____

But there is one thing Adam must not do if he is to remain in a leadership role. What is that? (Genesis 2:17)

____

____

Read Genesis 3:6, 23. In these two verses, what happened to Adam's leadership role?

____

____

As a leader, Adam was tempted. He gave in. He enjoyed momentary pleasure. This pleasure was followed by great loss. Now, back to Joseph.

Read Genesis 39:11-20. Where did Joseph end up after refusing Potiphar's wife?

____

In prison, Joseph interpreted a dream correctly (Genesis 40) and was noticed by Pharaoh who needed someone to interpret two disturbing dreams.

Read Genesis 41:41-44. Describe Joseph's new state of affairs.

____

____

____

____

As a leader, Joseph was tempted, too. He didn't give in, but as a result, he endured pain, loneliness, and humiliation. All this, however, was followed by a greater leadership role.

In Lesson One, we talked about the problem of taking shortcuts to get where we're going. The shortcut temptation is big for leaders. But saying yes to a shortcut, as Adam did, weakens leadership; saying no as Joseph did strengthens it.

Read Luke 4:1-14. Jesus, the greatest leader the world will ever know, was tempted. What were his choices?

(v. 4) ____

(v. 8) ____

(v. 12) ____

Following this refusal to give in, Jesus began his ministry in the power of the Spirit. What does all this say to you personally?

____

____

____

____

Everyone is called to leadership. Select your form(s) of leadership from the list below and describe your role in each.

Church ___________________________________

Parish ___________________________________

Family ___________________________________

Community _______________________________

Civic ____________________________________

Prayer ___________________________________

Moral ___________________________________

Job _____________________________________

*

Read Mark 1:35, 6:46 and Luke 5:16, 6:12. Jesus has a divine nature; he is God's Son. What does he model for us in these Scriptures?

____

Why do you think Jesus needs to pray?

____

Read 1 Chronicals 29:11-12. Where does your strength as a leader come from?

____

Read 2 Chronicals 25:8. Where does your power as a leader come from?

____

As a leader, you will be tempted to go against what God has said and thereby weaken or forfeit your leadership position. The power and strength you need will come to you from God only as you pray for them.

*

One of a leader's biggest temptations is to abuse power.

Read John 13:5. Jesus modeled humility. How?

____

____

Read Luke 22:24-27. Jesus tells leaders how to act. What does he tell them?

____

____

A leader avoids power abuse by becoming a servant.

Read Isaiah 6:8. What are Isaiah's words to the Lord?

____

____

Knowing what it costs in right choices, prayer, and service, will these be your words, too?

Personal Application

Refer to the list of names in your home circle on page 27. Select from that list the names of people who are under your leadership or coleadership. List those names in the left column and write next to each one the ways you can be a servant to that person.

Name	**Service**
____________	______________________
____________	______________________
____________	______________________
____________	______________________

What temptations could weaken your leadership of these people?

____________ ______________________

____________ ______________________

____________ ______________________

____________ ______________________

Write out a prayer that you, as a leader, need to pray.

____

____

____

____

Your superego may have some ideas from past programming about what a leader "should" do and expect. Some of us have been led to believe that we can never be any kind of leader. Some believe that a leader has blind power to do what he or she wants. Some believe that a leader or coleader does not need to be a servant.

What are some of your past ideas about the meaning of leadership?

What are some of your new ideas about the meaning of leadership?

What is your leadership role in your community circle?

What are some of the temptations that could undo the work you have been given to do?

What is a prayer you will want to pray daily for yourself as a community leader?

____

____

____

____

Review the list of names in your global circle on page 27. Everything we do touches others in the Body of Christ. If we are moral, if we are prayerful, if we are servants in leadership, then our leadership generates good for every single person throughout the globe.

> *Summary:* Leadership is an awesome task. It means taking a stand for God's way—especially when tempted. It means praying for the strength that can only come from God. It means avoiding the power trap by becoming humble enough to serve others.

Wrap Up

Continue during the week: Tell a friend about a time when you were a servant to someone.

Gift Assessment Chart: In your current situation, what is the best way you can exercise the gift of leadership?

____

____

Copy this onto the Gift Assessment Chart on page 125. If you think this will bring healing to yourself or others, circle it.

Especially for you: Schedule a weekend retreat. Taking a retreat for a day or two is not be considered running away.

Just for fun: This lesson calls for a milk shake. Go ahead. Enjoy.

Journal: Write about a temptation in your life that you gave in to; explain the long-range results.

Memorize: "Then I heard the voice of the Lord saying, 'Whom shall I send? Who will go for us?' 'Here I am,' I said; 'send me!' " (Isaiah 6:8)

Closing Prayer

Dear God, I need your grace and strength and power to make the choices I need to make to be a leader for you.

Glory to the Father, and to the Son, and to the Holy Spirit; as it was in the beginning, is now, and will be for ever. Amen.

Lesson Eight
Evangelizing

Go into the whole world and proclaim the gospel to every creature.
Mark 16:15

Beginning Prayer

Dear God, I'm not a preacher. I don't know if I can carry out this lesson. Through your Holy Spirit, help me in the best way possible for me.

Glory to the Father, and to the Son, and to the Holy Spirit; as it was in the beginning, is now, and will be for ever. Amen.

The Lesson:
Telling Others What God Has Done

There is no better place to start than the most famous command of Jesus, the verse that has sent millions of willing people from the safety and comfort of their homes to the far and lonely byways of the world.

Read Matthew 28:18-20. These words of Jesus are reverently called the Great Commission. Another word for this Scripture is *evangelization.* It's the command to tell other people the Good News.

We used to think that evangelization was for missionaries, and our job was to have bake sales and raffles to support them. Now we hear that supporting missionaries is only part of our work. Here are words Pope Paul VI addressed to us in his apostolic exhortation titled *On Evangelization in the Modern World:* "The Gospel message...is indeed necessary. It is unique. It cannot be replaced. It does not permit either indifference, syncretism or accommodation. It is a question of people's salvation" (#5).

The difference between teaching and evangelizing is that Christian teaching shows people how to follow Jesus and live God's commands; evangelizing *brings* people to Jesus. In our families and communities, there may be people who once knew God's way and God's Son but have turned away for their own reasons. There may be others who have never known God's ways. If we've come to God at a later age, there may be a second family or younger children who have never heard about how much God loves us all. Perhaps there are coworkers or friends of our children who have no idea that there is more to life than they know. You and I can tell these people there is something more for them.

Read Luke 2:8-11. This is the account of a pretty awesome evangelist. The shepherds were just doing their jobs and getting on with their lives. Then who appears to them?

___

What is the angel's message?

___

___

___

Here is a model for our own evangelizing. We start with someone we know who is getting on with life and we say, "Let's go to lunch (or come for coffee). I have some good news to tell you."

Someone: ***(Seated at lunch)*** I'm really curious. What's the good news?

You: This is something I've kept to myself for a long time.

Someone: Really?

You: Yes, it's a little difficult for me because I've never done this before. I want to share something with you that's very important to me. I want you to know that I'm a Catholic and being a Catholic is a source of happiness to me. It has introduced me to Jesus. You're my friend who means a lot to me, and I'd like to tell you about it.

Someone: (1) That's something I'd like to hear about.

(2) Not today, okay?

(3) Hey, I'm a Catholic, too, but I don't go to church.

(4) I know you're a Catholic, and I've been meaning to ask you about it.

You: (1) I believe that Jesus loves me and cares about me and wants to be a part of my life. There's a lot to it. Could you come to church with me on Sunday (or to an information night) and meet our parish priest?

(2) Sure, but if you ever want to know more, I'm here.

(3) I'd love to hear your story. (*After listening.*) Things are so different now. Could you come with me to Mass on Sunday?

(4) Really? What do you want to ask?

Read Isaiah 40:9. Isaiah offers sage advice. Speaking through Isaiah, what does God say?

____

____

Read Isaiah 52:7. What encouraging words God provides for us through the prophet Isaiah! Consider the feet of someone trampling for months over rocky, dusty hillsides. We're talking caked-on dirt, jagged toenails, abrasions, and thick callouses. But because these feet bring "...glad tidings, announcing peace, bearing good news," they are called

____

What do you think God is saying to us about the way we look to him when we tell others about him?

____

____

Read Matthew 10:11-14. Evangelizing is not an easy task. There will be times of failure or, at least, times that look like failure.

Jesus' disciples were sent to teach with Jesus' words tucked firmly in their hearts. How were they sometimes received?

____

If your words are not well received, what will you do?

____

____

Keep trying perhaps?

I have a neighbor who has strongly resisted my attempts to share the Good News. But when her teenage daughter was in a critical accident, she came to get me. She grabbed my hand, held it all the way down the street, up the driveway, around the hedge, and into the front door. She pushed me into her daughter's room. "Pray," she commanded.

Read again Matthew 28:20. Evangelizing is a special and difficult task, but Jesus promises to help us. The help comes from Jesus who is with us always, even to

____

Read Luke 22:7-12. This story emphasizes the theme further. Jesus sent Peter and James to prepare the Last Supper. "When you go into the city, a man will meet you carrying a jar of water." (It was unheard of for men to carry water jugs, so this particular man was easily located.) The man led them to the upper room, which was all ready and furnished.

As an evangelist, you are like Peter and James preparing the Last Supper. Everything is arranged by God ahead of time; you have to do only your part.

Remember again these words of Jesus to his disciples: "I am with you." As you talk about him to someone else, you will not be alone.

Personal Application

Matthew 5:14 tells us to be a light to the world. Different personalities will be different kinds of light. Consider the purpose of:

a searchlight ___________________________________

a house light ____________________________________

a lighthouse light ________________________________

a sanctuary light _________________________________

Review the list of names in your home circle on page 27. What kind of light are you in your home circle?

____

____

What kind of a light would you like to be?

____

____

Matthew 5:13 tells us that we are to be salt to the world. Consider ways to make people in your home circle thirsty. How could you be like nourishment to them?

____

____

____

Following is a true story about evangelizing in a home circle.

Jean: ***(Working in garden)*** Dear God, please help me to tell someone about you today.
God: Okay.
Dolores: ***(Jean's adult daughter)*** Mom, before I leave, do you have something to say to me?
Jean: Yes, but how did you know?
Dolores: I don't know. I just had a feeling.

Jean:	I want to tell you that God really loves you and wants your love in return.
Dolores:	But, Mom, Christians are so boring.
Jean:	Honey, look around you at the colors and variety in all the animals and flowers. God isn't boring.
Dolores:	Hmmm. Maybe not. I'll think about it.

Write a possible conversation between you and someone in your home circle.

You____

Him/Her ____________________________________

You____

Him/Her ____________________________________

You____

Him/Her ____________________________________

You____

Telling the Good News "off the cuff" may be too difficult to do. Preparation will lead the way. Think about a time in your life when:

God came through in a crisis for you.

____

____

You knew Jesus loved you.

____

____

You experienced God's presence.

____

____

Review the list of names in your community circle on page 27. Think of a person in your community circle who doesn't seem to know about God's love and care.

____

Write an account of how you experienced God in your life. Write it so that you can tell it to someone in one or two minutes.

____

____

____

____

____

Before you actually tell your story to someone, I encourage you with the following story.

Once there was a five-year-old boy whose mother brought him to a concert by Paderewski. The child somehow climbed on the stage, seated himself at the grand piano, and began to play "Twinkle, Twinkle Little Star." Just as his embarrassed mother began to whisk the child away, the great Paderewski came on stage and said, "Leave the lad alone." To the boy he said, "Keep playing." As the little fingers played the simple melody, Paderewski sat beside the child and began playing the bass, filling in with chords and arpeggios. Paderewski then reached around the child with his right hand and supplied the libretto.

They say that the applause was thunderous. As the years went by, no one remembered what Paderewski had performed. But all could remember "Twinkle, Twinkle Little Star."

As you tell your story, you are that child at the piano. It's the Holy Spirit who slips his presence around you and supplies the chords and libretto. You only have to tell your story and leave the rest to God's perfect timing.

Review the list of names in your global circle on page 27. How could you bring the Good News to them and around the world? Is there someone in your global circle to whom you could send a Bible? What else comes to mind?

____

____

____

For some of you, this may have been a heavy lesson. Perhaps you're uncomfortable with evangelizing. Understand that evangelizing to avoid feeling guilty is not a good reason for sharing the Good News. Evangelizing, like other ways of reaching out, needs to come from your heart. Do only what your heart tells you to do. The words that you really want to share, no matter how small, will do more than a lot of words that come only from the guilty voice of your superego. God bless you.

> *Summary:* To tell someone the Good News of Jesus' love is to be a part of the Great Commission. It can be risky: we might be rejected. On the other hand, we might bring light where there was no light. In whatever way we respond, we are not alone.

Wrap Up

Continue during the week: Tell a friend the story you wrote about how you experienced God in your life (see page 95).

Gift Assessment Chart: In your current situation, how can you best exercise the gift of evangelization?

___

___

Copy this onto the Gift Assessment Chart on page 125. If you think this will bring healing to yourself or others, circle it.

Especially for you: What would fill you with God's love? Mass at the convent? a quiet day away? reading the Acts of the Apostles or the life of Saint Francis? going to a prayer meeting? sitting on a beach? Whatever it is, go for it.

Just for fun: Pack a picnic and have dinner in the park (even if it's cold) or take your McDonald's dinner to a viewpoint.

Journal: Write about your greatest fear in telling someone else about God's love. Isn't it good that we can talk honestly to God.

Memorize: "Go into the whole world and proclaim the gospel to every creature" (Mark 16:15).

Closing Prayer

Dear God, thank you for all the ways you tell me about your love. I ask for the grace I need to tell others about you.

Glory to the Father, and to the Son, and to the Holy Spirit; as it was in the beginning, is now, and will be for ever. Amen.

Lesson Nine
Mercy

Be merciful, just as [also] your Father is merciful.

Luke 6:36

Beginning Prayer

Dear God, just as I stand in need of your mercy, please show me, through your Holy Spirit, how to be merciful to others.

Glory to the Father, and to the Son, and to the Holy Spirit; as it was in the beginning, is now, and will be for ever. Amen.

The Lesson: What It Means to Be Merciful

Our older children had been in a skit where they acted out the parable of the Good Samaritan. After a day at Granny's house on the island, we were driving down the ferry ramp on our way home.

That's when I saw her, a weary-looking woman carrying a baby and two shopping bags and holding on to a two-year-old. My heart went out to her. "Bill, can we stop?"

She and her baby scooted into the front seat beside me and my baby. The kids in the back seat scrunched over a little to make room for the two-year-old. I don't remember if we took her to the bus or to her home, but she was deeply grateful for the ride. As the car doors closed behind her, our children burst out with excited exclamations: "We were good samaritans!" And so we had been, in more ways than one, as we will see a little later.

*

My friend Rita told me about a young woman in our parish who was in desperate need. Rita works at the rectory, and the woman had come there asking for food. Both Rita and I were moved by her circumstances. Instead of giving her just the food she asked for, we helped her with clothing, furniture, and other things. Without realizing it, however, we greatly complicated the woman's life.

All she had wanted was food for a few days and the right to come back and ask for more later on. Her boyfriend sold the clothing and furniture to support his drug habit.

The woman was desolate over the loss of her new things. She was also worried about what Rita and I would think when we saw everything gone from her apartment. When we dropped by to visit with her, she wouldn't let us in—we who had been her only friends. Although we didn't realize it right away, we had made it difficult for her to come and ask for more food.

How could we have known that we were complicating that woman's situation? I realize now that we could have asked her how we could help and then listened to her answer. We started as good samaritans, touched by her pain, but we ended up acting out of our own need "to do something."

*

My friend Melody tells of a time when her daughter brought home a homeless teenager from school. Melody, who has a merciful heart, asked the girl to stay, even though there were a number of indications that this wasn't a good idea. In time, the situation involving a male family member became so intolerable that every day the girl stayed was a nightmare for Melody. In the end, the girl, now further wounded, had to go.

Mercy is a wonderful gift but, as many merciful people eventually discover, it needs to be wisely ministered.

*

Read Luke 10:29-37. Jesus uses the parable of the Good Samaritan to teach about mercy. Although this is a parable, let's assume that Jesus' listeners knew that it was possible to be mugged along the road between Jericho and Jerusalem. Certainly on those barren, twisted pathways, where bandits waited in ambush, there were many such muggings.

In Jesus' story, which of the many who might have been victimized in these hills did the Good Samaritan have mercy on?

____

In the Good Samaritan's travels, this was the one particular man whose situation touched his heart. Therefore, this man was his focus.

Read Matthew 20:29-34. Where was Jesus on his journey?

____

Who did he happen to meet? ______________________

What did they need?____________________________

How was Jesus affected? _________________________

This is one of the hallmarks of genuine mercy. The response comes from the heart and is not an "I should" action.

Read Mark 1:39-41. Where was Jesus going?

____

Who knelt in front of him and what did he want?

____

How did Jesus respond?

____

Why was Jesus moved to compassion by this particular leper?

____

____

Read Luke 7:11-15. Contrast this story with the one above. Again, Jesus is on a journey, but there are differences? How does the woman's behavior differ from the lepers'?

____

____

What is the same about Jesus' response?

____

Whenever we act with true mercy, it's because in one way or another we tune into and share someone else's pain.

Read Luke 8:26-39. This time Jesus encounters a man in great need. What does the healed man ask of Jesus?

(v. 38) ____

____

What does Jesus tell him to do instead?

____

____

Go back to the Good Samaritan story in Luke 10. Read verses 30-35 very carefully. What was the Good Samaritan doing when he came upon the wounded man?

____

What did the Good Samaritan do after he took the wounded man to the inn?

(v. 35)____

He didn't stick around. He rescued the man and continued on his own journey.

Jesus doesn't tell us that caring for the victim became the Samaritan's life's work. Nor did the Samaritan consider himself the solution to the victim's life-problems. The Samaritan didn't create an agenda for the victim to follow (and therefore he wasn't let down when the victim didn't follow it). Simply put, the Good Samaritan's heart was touched, and he was merciful to the suffering person he met while on his journey.

Jesus' entire life gave this example. Touched with compassion, Jesus healed many people. Then he sent them to the priests, to their homes, and in the case of the widow, back to her son. He touched their lives with mercy and went on his way.

Personal Application

How about your journey? Where are you going? We are not talking about a spiritual journey in this lesson but about the daily mission to which you are called.

For many years, my daily journey was getting a houseful of children up each morning to be cared for and guided through the day. In journey-language, I was a shepherdess leading my flock of rambunctious lambs and kids to the pasture each day and safely home again at night.

Review the list of names in your home circle on page 27. With these people in mind, describe your home journey as it relates to coming across wounded people. If you want, use journey-language (analogy) to help clarify your role.

Who might be the victims you come across who need your mercy? (Once one of my daughters came home from school too stricken with grief to cry. The part in the school play had gone to someone else. I could feel all her pain.)

How do you bandage the wounds of the people in your home? (With my daughter the only thing I could do was sit beside her while she cried. I couldn't possibly say the right thing. I couldn't take away the hurt. It was unthinkable for me to call the drama teacher and find out why...although I thought of it.)

Name	Bandage

Review the list of names in your community circle on page 27. Describe your community journey in terms of the wounded people there.

___

___

___

Who are the victims along your community journey?

| ___ | ___ |
| ___ | ___ |

How do you bandage the wounds of these people?

Name	**Bandage**
___	___
___	___
___	___
___	___

Carefully consider the bandages you've listed above. In front of each example of a bandaged wound, place a "V" (values) if you are genuinely acting in mercy or an "S" (superego) if you feel you are acting from that internal voice that says, "I should."

Is there anything you have decided to do differently or not to do at all in order to be true to who you are?

___

___

___

Review the list of names in your global circle on page 27. How can you bring mercy to victims elsewhere in the world? A phone call to a senator on behalf of someone suffering or a donation of blood comes to my mind. What comes to yours?

____

____

____

Summary: As we travel through life, we will come across many people in need of mercy. The mercy we show them is most authentic when it comes from our heart. After we have participated in a merciful way in their suffering, we need to continue on with the journey already set before us.

Keep in mind that there are times when it may be appropriate to stop mid-journey and take the other fork in the road. For example, perhaps you've helped care for a child born with AIDS but are beginning to see a need to start a group that will reach out with compassion to many more of these needy children. Great ministries have begun this way—so have great failures. The really merciful person will need the help of others to launch such a project. Listen carefully to your inner voices. Which voices are directing you? The work arising from the superego is exhausting. The work arising from the inspiration of the Holy Spirit and a God-inspired value system brings joy.

Wrap Up

Continue during the week: Think about past experiences of offering either excessive or inadequate mercy. Where did you succeed and where did you fail? Share this with a friend but don't let any failures worry you. We learn from experience.

Gift Assessment Chart: In your current situation, how can you best exercise the gift of mercy?

___

___

Copy this onto the Gift Assessment Chart on page 126. If you think this will bring healing to yourself or others, circle it.

Especially for you: Be merciful to yourself. Who is hardest on you? your spouse? your boss? your roommate? you? Write a letter to yourself from that person and show great mercy to yourself.

Just for fun: Buy two doughnuts, two bags of popcorn, or two pomegranates and share them with someone.

Journal: Write about a time you needed mercy. Write about what you would do if you met someone today with that same need.

Memorize: "Be merciful, just as [also] your Father is merciful" (Luke 6:36).

Closing Prayer

Dear God, thank you for your mercy to me, especially when I have least deserved it. Please give me the grace to be merciful to others.

Glory to the Father, and to the Son, and to the Holy Spirit; as it was in the beginning, is now, and will be for ever. Amen.

Lesson Ten
Praying

Ask and it will be given to you; seek and you will find; knock and the door will be opened to you.

Matthew 7:7

Beginning Prayer

Dear God, let your Holy Spirit pray through me for my friends.

Glory to the Father, and to the Son, and to the Holy Spirit; as it was in the beginning, is now, and will be for ever. Amen.

The Lesson:
Prayer Works

In the rearing of my family, there were many times when the problems and the tasks of the day were beyond my ability. I'd done my best—and it wasn't enough. On my knees beside my bed was the one and only solution.

Here are prayers and answers I remember clearly.

"Dear God, this kid's temper tantrums are destroying me and him. Help me. Help him."

I heard these words, "Pat, will you trust me?"

The next time that particular kid stomped into the kitchen

and blew up, I said nothing aloud. Under my breath I prayed, "I will trust you, Lord." I said it eight times and smiled at the perpetrator.

In just a short while of trusting silently, the temper tantrums ceased.

Trust in the LORD with all your heart,
on your own intelligence rely not....

Proverbs 3:5

*

"Dear God, her situation breaks my heart. I've told her that her plans are going against what you have said, but she doesn't hear. Now there's only one thing to do. Here, Lord, look at me. I'm making a little basket with my hands. I put her in it, and I'm giving this basket to you. From now on, I will thank you each day for what you are doing in her life, no matter what the circumstances look like."

The answer was many years in coming but it came.

Pray without ceasing. In all circumstances give thanks,
for this is the will of God for you in Christ Jesus.

1 Thessalonians 5:17-18

*

"Dear God, I'm really scared. This child is getting sicker and sicker every day. Help us. Help the doctor."

All who call upon me I will answer;
I will be with them in distress;
I will deliver them and give them honor.

Psalm 91:15

*

"Dear God, he's in jail, and I know the problem has a name: alcoholism. We need a miracle, dear God. We need you."

When you look for me, you will find me. Yes, when you seek me with all your heart, you will find me with you, says the LORD*....*

Jeremiah 29:13-14

*

"Dear God, what am I going to do with her?"

"Apologize."

"Me? But, Lord..."

"You're to blame, too."

I sat beside her bed. "Honey, I'm sorry I was so cross."

"Mom, I'm sorry, too."

Show me favor; hear my prayer.

Psalm 4:2

*

"Dear God, my coworker is involved with a married woman. I'm going to pray for him, using the words of Scripture. I don't know what else to do."

Put to death, then, the parts of you that are earthly: immorality, impurity, passion, evil desire, and the greed that is idolatry.

Colossians 3:5

*

"Dear God, the new priest asked for prayer. Please show me a Scripture I can pray for him daily."

Let the word of Christ dwell in you richly, as in all wisdom you teach and admonish one another....And whatever you do, in word or in deed, do everything in the name of the Lord Jesus, giving thanks to God the Father through him.

Colossians 3:16-17

*

A leader of the Church was in prison and his friends were greatly worried. They gathered together and began to pray, probably something like this: "Oh, God, release our brother. Jesus, our friend, save this leader we know you love." While they were praying, something remarkable happened.

Read Acts 12:5-16. How were the prayers of the prisoner's friends answered?

____

How did Peter's friends respond?

(v. 15)____

(v. 16)____

Can you blame them?

As much as we hear about prayer, we still forget that prayers are answered. We've never done "everything" we can possibly do to reach out to our friends: we can always pray. We can pray for them, and we can expect answers to our prayers.

Read Luke 11:5-8. Jesus makes an interesting point about prayer. What is necessary in order to get certain prayers answered?

____

____

____

____

Read Luke 11:9-10. What are three ways of being persistent?

__________________ and it will ____________________

__________________ and you will __________________

__________________ and the ______________________

Read Luke 18:1-7. Why did Jesus tell this parable?

(v. 1) ____

What did the widow do?

____

What was the judge's response?

____

Let's say that you and three friends are deeply concerned over a mutual friend. "If only Jesus could help him," you say to one another. "If only we could take him on a mat and lower him through a roof to Jesus." What do you do instead?

____

____

Your friend's situation is not better. So what do you do?

____

____

Still there is no improvement. What do you do? (Refer again to Luke 11:9.)

____

____

You can expect an answer consistent with the character of God. It may not be your answer, but it will be a right answer. You will have the peaceful knowledge that you were faithful to what you could do.

Who are we to pray for?

2 Timothy 2:1-2 ________________________________

2 Chronicles 7:14 ________________________________

James 5:13________________________________

James 5:15________________________________

Matthew 5:44 ________________________________

Ephesians 6:18 ________________________________

What are we to pray for?

Ephesians 1:18 ________________________________

Psalm 122:6________________________________

Philippians 1:9 ________________________________

Philippians 4:6 ________________________________

Ephesians 6:20 ________________________________

It's never too late to pray. There is nothing we can't talk over with God. Nothing is too big or too little for God's concern.

Yet, God's answers are not always our answers. God's plan is wider and broader and more full of healing than our plans. What God asks is prayer that perseveres, trusts, and waits. What God gives is an answer permeated with love.

There is no other way to help others that compares with praying for God's blessing and intervention for them. Prayer is our strength in all things. It is prayer that brings heaven down to earth and changes the courses of events.

Personal Application

Review the list of names in your home circle on page 27. Is there someone in your home circle whose situation is tenuous, heartbreaking, or dangerous? Pray now for that person?

> Father, here is *(name of person in your home circle).* There is nothing more I can do. I place ____________ in your hands and ask you to take over with love. I thank you, Lord, right now for your answer and your loving plan. I come to you in Jesus' name. Amen.

If you are desperate enough to do something that may feel a little silly, make a basket of your hands and place that person in the basket. Lift the basket up toward God.

> Dear God, here is *(name of person in your home circle).* I thank you for taking ____________ out of my hands and into yours. Amen.

Review the list of names in your community circle on page 27. What is going on in your community that needs your prayers? Is your pastor looking weary? Is your legislature ungodly? Are there topless bars that need to be shut down? Are your friends fighting among themselves? Is someone you know drinking or doing drugs? Is there anyone bearing the suffering of rejection? Ask in prayer:

> *Dear God,*
> *What situation do you want me to pray for?*
>
> ____

How should I pray?

____

____

Record today's date so you can remember when you started praying for this situation. ___________________________

Don't let your superego talk you into praying for lots and lots of people and problems. "I should pray for…" is not the same as knowing who God especially wants you to pray for.

Review the list of names in your global circle on page 27. What specific global concern do you think God wants you to pray for? One of my prayers is for the emotional healing of women who have had abortions. What is one of yours?

____

____

____

____

____

Summary: Prayer is *the* great help we give to others. We call out to God with strong persistence and trust God to hear and answer.

Wrap Up

Continue during the week: Share with a friend your persistent prayer for someone.

Gift Assessment Chart: In your current situation, how can you best exercise the gift of prayer?

____

____

Copy this onto the Gift Assessment Chart on page 126. If you think this will bring healing to yourself or others, circle it.

Especially for you: Go to your favorite quiet place. Today is the day to pray for you. It will take some time, but that's okay. Talk to God about your childhood. Thank God for the happy times and talk about the sad, lonely, terrible, or shameful times. Listen to God responding to you, comforting you, encouraging you.

Move on to your teenage years. Talk to God about them; tell God everything you need to say. Listen to God responding to you, supporting you, loving you. Move on to the years since then. You have a listening Friend. Tell God about your joys, sorrows, and regrets. Thank God for making you. Ask God to show you what you need to confess. Ask God to forgive you. Ask God to guide you. Let God's love surround you.

Close by telling God how much you need him and that you love him.

Just for fun: Take a cup of cocoa outside at midnight, sit on the steps, and count the stars.

Journal: Write about the time when an important prayer seemed to go unanswered.

Memorize: "Ask and it will be given to you; seek and you will find; knock and the door will be opened to you" (Matthew 7:7).

Closing Prayer

Dear God, I need the grace to persevere faithfully in prayer. I know that this only comes from you.

Glory to the Father, and to the Son, and to the Holy Spirit; as it was in the beginning, is now, and will be for ever. Amen.

Guidelines for Starting a "Listening" Group

The basic characteristic of a listening support group is "safety." An effective support group is a place where people in pain feel "safe" to share their past experiences and realize healing in the sharing of their stories.

The following guidelines will direct your efforts to begin a "safe" and effective listening support group.

- Limit the size of the group. Six to eight persons is a large enough group to allow for a diversity of backgrounds and experiences while keeping the group small enough to allow for personal attention and supportive listening.
- Do not make a public announcement regarding the group's meeting place and time. Once the group is formed, keep all meetings "closed." Welcoming new members may be a courteous gesture, but it keeps the dynamics within the group in a constant state of flux. The group as a "safe" place is threatened.
- Develop a timetable. Decide how many times the group will meet (six, eight, ten) and what the focus will be for each meeting.
- Do not get someone from the helping professions to facilitate the group. The group is not designed to do

professional work. The group's function is to listen with attentive care.

- Ask for a reassurance from each member in the group to keep confidential all that goes on in the group. This is one more element that adds to the sense of "safety" for the members.
- The support group is not an advisory group. Its purpose is to listen, empathize, and care. Open and close each session with an "emotional check": an opportunity for each member to briefly state, in a word or sentence, how he/she is feeling.
- At the end of the six, eight, or ten sessions (determined at the outset), direct the group in a review of the previous weeks. At that time, decide to disband, regroup (allowing new members), or continue as a closed group. If the group decides to disband or regroup, allow one full final session for closure.

Gift Assessment Chart

Lesson Two: How can I best reach out to others with the gift of hospitality?

____

____

____

____

Lesson Three: How can I best reach out to others with the gift of encouragement?

____

____

____

____

Lesson Four: How can I best reach out to others with the gift of giving?

____

____

____

____

Lesson Five: How can I best reach out to others with the gift of teaching?

____

____

____

____

Lesson Six: How can I best reach out to others with the gift of listening?

____

____

____

____

Lesson Seven: How can I best reach out to others with the gift of leadership?

____

____

____

____

Lesson Eight: How can I best reach out to others with the gift of evangelizing?

____

____

____

____

Lesson Nine: How can I best reach out to others with the gift of mercy?

____

____

____

____

Lesson Ten: How can I best reach out to others with the gift of praying?

____

____

____

____

Which Is Your Strongest Gift?

Look over the assessments of gifts that enable you to reach out to others.

Which of your gifts give you the most joy?

____________________ ____________________

____________________ ____________________

Which of your gifts do you perform the best?

____________________ ____________________

____________________ ____________________

Which of your gifts are the easiest for you to give?

____________________ ____________________

____________________ ____________________

When you reach out to others, what are you doing when time seems to “fly by”?

____________________ ____________________

____________________ ____________________

If someone asks you how you best reach out to others, what will you reply?

____

____

____

____

Other Helpful Books by Pat King...

Help for Woman With Too Much to Do

This invaluable book shows today's overextended women how a change in lifestyle, outlook, and expectations can help them face life's demands with renewed vigor. *$3.95*

Scripture-Based Solutions to Handling Stress

Those who feel trapped in a stress-filled downward spiral will find help in this book as its hands-on workbook approach helps readers take charge of their lives and defeat feelings of helplessness and exhaustion. *$4.95*

Also, a guide to the Word of God...

A Catholic Guide to the Bible

by Father Oscar Lukefahr, C.M.

Written to help those who feel drawn to the Bible, but who are also somewhat intimidated by it, this book "takes readers by the hand" and gently guides them through the Bible. For each of the seventy-three biblical books, the author offers pertinent historical background, information about the biblical author and the literary style of the work, and a theological interpretation of selected passages. *$5.95*
(Workbook available—$2.95)